Postcards from Arundel
1900–1930

Claire Seymour

S.B. Publications

For Bryan and Barbara, for their unfailing support,
encouragement and love over the years;
and for Chris, for introducing me to Arundel
and for continuing to share the dream.

Edited by David Arscott at Pomegranate Press.

Cover Design by EH Graphics Tel: 01273 515527

British Library Cataloguing-in-Publication Data.
A catalogue record for this book is available from the British Library.

ISBN 1–85770–295–6

First published in 2004 by S.B. Publications, 19 Grove Road, Seaford,
East Sussex BN25 1TP. Tel: 01323 893498

Printed by Ethos Productions Ltd.

Contents

Acknowledgements

This book would not have been possible without the help and support of many people. My thanks to the staff at Arundel Library and Chichester Records Office for their expertise in providing source material; to Arundel Museum, for being a source of information and inspiration; to Barbara Seymour for tireless finding new and interesting postcards to add to the book; to those friends and family who encouraged the project with their constant enthusiasm (Louise Seymour, Sandra Watson, Albert Seymour, Anna Bunney, Sophie Duncan, John Walkley, Rebecca Pritchard, Paul Deegan, Mac Wenham and Matt Smith); to Chris Cooper for his unquestioning faith in this project and my ability to deliver it; and to Bryan Seymour, who spent countless hours devising and laying out the orginal pages, transforming the text and pictures into a visually pleasing book.

Introduction

A n historic town with an imposing castle, set among rolling countryside and flanked by the River Arun, Arundel has been described as the 'jewel in the crown' of its district. As well as its physical attractions, Arundel has a rich history as a busy port, thriving marketplace and lively town.

A view of the High Street, posted on August 26, 1911.

The streets and buildings preserve this history for the benefit of visitors and townspeople alike. The town has a seemingly timeless quality, yet look closely and change can be seen all around. For the most part, the new has been skilfully blended with the old, creating a tapestry that incorporates both ancient and modern strands.

Visitors to Arundel have long appreciated the many varied but complementary aspects that make up the town. Tourism started to make an impact from the 18th century onwards when visitors to the fashionable seaside resorts of Brighton and Bognor took day trips to Arundel to admire the scenery and look at the castle.

The castle, which opened more frequently from the 1800s onwards, recorded just over 1,100 visitors in 1857. In 1864, a year after the railway line and station at Arundel opened, the number rose to almost 17,000.

Tourism was encouraged by the opening of the railway line and the expansion in stagecoach and, later, bus services. The gradual increase in leisure time and the rising standards of living meant that growing numbers of people were able to visit the town.

Arundel responded to this burgeoning tourist trade by providing hotels, inns, tea rooms and souvenirs. From the early 1900s, the introduction of postcards, which were relatively cheap to buy and send, meant that people could easily share their experiences with others. Newsagents and stationers welcomed this new invention by producing their own postcards.

A postcard of August 13 1902. Early cards like this had a space for the message on the front, and only the address was permitted on the back.

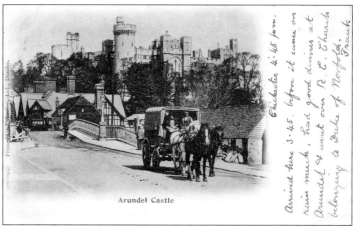

Arundel Castle

The first view of Arundel for visitors arriving at the railway station early in the 20th century.

2   ARUNDEL. — *View from the Railway.* — I.L.

Dear Win

Fine down here today. Just waiting for the Brighton train, 11.20. Very pretty little place. Hope all goes well.

Love from Harold

24 May 1915

Charcoal burners shown in Arundel Park early in the 20th century.

Those included here all date from that period. Wherever possible their messages have been included, since these often enhance their interest, providing a snapshot of history and an insight into the past.

This book is not intended to be either a complete history or a comprehensive guide to Arundel. The appeal of this wonderful selection of postcards is that it illustrates so many and various aspects of this attractive town and provides an array of fleeting yet memorable glimpses into its past.

The hospital in King Street was set up in the early 1900s as an 'emergency' hospital. It was converted to residential use after a new hospital was built on the Chichester Road in the early 1930s.

River Arun

Winding its way up from the coast at Littlehampton,
the Arun provided leisure and work for many

Throughout the centuries, the fast-flowing Arun has provided a livelihood for the people of the town. Eels, pike, bass and grey mullet were among the fish found in the river. The grey mullet in particular was praised for its flavour, and Arundel was renowned for its banquets at which the fish was served.

In the 17th century the writer of *The High Stream of Arundel* claimed that the Arundel mullet was 'the best and fattest in England, and of a most pleasing taste'. In the late 18th and early 19th centuries mullet was sold locally to hotels such as the Norfolk Arms, as well as being sent to London. In the late 19th and early 20th centuries some of the hotels offered fishing trips on the river for their guests.

When Arundel's slaughterhouses were at their peak they tipped their waste into the river, which led to an abundance of eels. These were caught using a long pole with lengths of wool attached to one end. Worms were threaded onto the wool, and as the eels ate the worms the wool got caught in their teeth. The pole was then lifted clear of the water and shaken hard to dislodge the eels.

Fish are still caught in the river today, including the mullet which gives its name to those born in Arundel.

View of the river, looking towards the town.

Arundel from the River,

Boat trip from Littlehampton to Arundel. Photographers would race to have the developed pictures ready by the time the boat reached its destination.

Dear Harold,
Just off to Arundel on this boat,
please find us.
Love from Leslie
Littlehampton, 8 Aug 1919

St Philips church (it later became the cathedral) from the river. The postcard makers note that the church 'holds out a curious contrast to the old houses standing between it and the river.'

Dear Rose,
Have just arrived. Lovely weather. Am just
off for a long walk & a long drink. Wish
you could join me. It is very pretty scenery
& at present everything looks beautiful.

With love, Alex
2 July 1910

5

Along the Arun

From the beginning of Arundel's development the river played an important role in trade and industry

Barges like this were used for carrying goods along the river and for unloading cargo from the larger sailing ships.

Arundel from the Railway   5809

Beside the river was a good spot for Arundel's windmills as they had access to water and, being sited away from the town, were able to make full use of any wind blowing along the Arun.

The windmill at the end of Fitzalan Road was built in 1830, and from the early 1840s onwards was used by the Bartlett family for

A view from the Black Rabbit inn looking upstream towards Amberley, which had a number of industries centred on the chalk pits and the river.

EW FROM BLACK RABBIT ARUNDEL.   511

This mill was used in the 19th century for grinding corn. It has now been converted into a house, but much of its original form has been retained.

grinding corn. It was damaged during a storm in 1915 and gradually fell into disrepair. It was then converted into a house. Further upriver, at Portreeves Acre, a windmill was in existence by the first part of the 18th century. The site continued to be used until the end of the 19th century.

Dear Mother,

Sorry I have been unable to write to you before. The key is in the small drawer of the dressing table. I think I shall stay for 10 days if not I shall be home on Sunday.

Love to you all, Edgar, 29 July 1909

The mill at Portreeves Acre, used for making cement in the 19th century, was destroyed later that century.

The Port

For centuries the port was at the heart of Arundel life, bringing trade and wealth to the town.

A view of the port showing the various wharves and warehouses. The building to the right of the ships and bridge is the corn store.

Arundel, View from Wharf.

For hundreds of years the port was a key feature of Arundel. The town exported cattle, timber, corn, wool and lime and imported a range of goods including coal, wine, brandy and glass.

The port brought prosperity to Arundel and stamped its character on the town. Along the river were the buildings and trades needed to service the port – wharves, shipyards, docks, timber and coal yards and warehouses.

In the streets nearby were builders, boat makers, corn and coal merchants and brewers, as well as inns and loding houses for the sailors and other workers drawn to the port and growing town.

The pub names, with their maritime references, reflected the importance of the port: The Victory, The Jolly Sailor, The Ship and The Ship and Lighter.

About 1890, W.H. Chase described the town as 'a busy little place . . . Two considerable breweries were in action, as well as a timber yard, soap works and stream and windmills'.

As large sailing ships had difficulty navigating the narrow, winding river, most were towed in and out of the port by small boats or tugs. One of the most well known sights along the river was the paddle steamer Jumna, which towed vessels up to 200 tons.

The steam tug Jumna can be seen towing the sailing ship Alroy into the port.

Trade peaked in the 1820s when the port was home to 45 ships, some of which had been built in the town. The port declined from the 1840s onwards as Littlehampton developed as the premier port of the Arun. In 1864 the customs house moved from Arundel to Littlehampton. By the early 20th century the number of vessels entering Arundel had fallen dramatically.

In 1938 the railway bridge at Ford was built, thus preventing masted vessels getting to Arundel. With the decline of the port, the wharves and the quays along the river fell into disuse and the land was mostly developed for residential use.

Barges and ships used the wooden pier in the foreground to unload coal for the gasworks in Ford Road.

The Bridge

Over the centuries the bridge has often been replaced and rebuilt, sometimes causing misunderstandings and damage

This painting of the bridge shows the cantilevered footpath that was added in the 1830s.

The picture at the top of the page shows it as it looks today.

In 1724, the wooden bridge across the river was replaced, for the first time, with a stone bridge with three arches. In the early 1830s it was repaired and widened, and a footpath was added on either side. William Holmes, the mayor at the time, thought that the Arundel Savings Bank had agreed to fund the work out of a small surplus that it had.

After much disagreement and a legal battle, Holmes discovered that this was not the case and he had to pay the costs of the work and the legal fees. As a sour comment on this, Holmes added an inscription to the bridge that read, 'Be true and just in all your dealings'.

Looking across the bridge towards Queen Street. On the right is the Bridge Hotel and on the left is Herington and Son Ltd, 'draper and outfitter, milliner, dressmaker and tailor'.

Tom Buller's cottage, shown on the bridge, was allegedly used by smugglers who brought goods up the Arun. It was demolished in the 1930s.

In 1935, the stone bridge was replaced with a concrete one by West Sussex County Council. During the work, the river was diverted along the south bank by means of a dam. The strength of the water being channelled along the bank was so strong that it undermined the foundations of the Bridge Hotel, which had to be demolished.

Despite the damage they had caused, a bronze plaque to the engineers who built the new bridge was added once it was completed. Holmes's inscription and a Latin one commemorating the opening of the original stone bridge were also incorporated and both can be seen today.

Queen Street

Providing access to the town
via the bridge, the street was home
to both industry and commerce

The Bridge Hotel was built at the beginning of the 19th century. In about 1900, the hotel was described as having 'a spacious dining room with a balcony commanding a fine view of the castle-crowned woods, the town, and the river'. The proprietor, L. Gordon Burrell, also offered visitors 'billiards, carriages for hire, good stabling', boat trips and fishing.

As well as the Bridge Hotel, Queen Street had two pubs, the General Abercrombie and the White Hart.

The Swallow Brewery chimney can be seen on the right, behind the Bridge Hotel.

In 1935, during work on the new bridge, the hotel's foundations were undermined and it collapsed. A new hotel with a river terrace and tea gardens was built on the site shortly afterwards. This was replaced in the late 1980s with a block of flats.

The Constable family started the Swallow Brewery at the beginning of the 19th century. A century later, C.S. Constable advertised himself as a 'Pale Ale and Stout Brewer, Wine and Spirit Merchant'.

Later in the 20th century, Constable joined forces with the Henty family, who ran Henty's Bank in the town, and the business was renamed Henty and Constable. The brewery was pulled down in the 1930s. The brewery's advertising symbol, a large wooden swallow, was saved and placed on top of the town hall, where it stands today. The site was used for a cinema and, later still, for a petrol station.

As well as the Swallow Brewery, the Constable family ran the Anchor Brewery in Littlehampton. Herington's shop is on the right. The single storey building next to it is the 'old wattle' house, used for storing the sheep pen hurdles for the cattle market.

Bridge House (16 Queen Street) was built in 1772 for the manager of the Swallow Brewery, which stood on the opposite side of the road. It later became a drapers run by Mr Levett. In 1860, it was taken over by Alfred and John Herington, who established their own drapery, millinery and tailoring business.

In 1900, Herington's could boast that they always had 'a large and Well-Assorted Stock of Drapery to select from', and that they were 'Special makers in Ladies' and Children's Underclothing, Corsets etc'. The firm was in business until the early 1970s. A few years later, Bridge House was converted into a hotel.

High Street

The focus of daily life, the High Street
offered goods and services for both
townspeople and visitors

With its steep road leading to the cathedral and parish church, the High Street has long been the focus for the town and its people. As well as providing a place for commerce and business, the street has also witnessed numerous scenes of remembrance and celebration over the years.

The road seems to have been called the High Street from the early 13th century onwards. It was also called New Market Street from the late 18th century when the market moved from Maltravers Street to the High Street.

Like Maltravers Street, the High Street has always formed one of the town's principal thoroughfares. Whereas Maltravers Street developed predominantly as a residential area, the High Street was, and still is, primarily a road of shops, pubs, hotels, banks and restaurants. When tourism began to develop from the early 19th century onwards, it was ideally placed to offer visitors a wide range of services.

The mixture of different architectural styles illustrates how the High Street continually developed throughout its history as buildings were modified or replaced. Beneath some impressive exteriors, older buildings are often preserved, some of them dating back more than 400 years.

A view looking down the High Street. Both cyclists in the picture have chosen to walk rather than cycle up the road.

High Street, Arundel

An artist's impression from 1828, showing the top end of the High Street, opposite Maltravers Street. The Bartlett family, whose shop is shown, were corn merchants and millers. In the middle of the 19th century these houses were demolished during work to extend the castle grounds, and a wall was built in their place.

On the corner of the High Street and Mill Road, facing the river, is the post office. The 15th duke commissioned this building in 1892, after he was he was appointed her majesty's postmaster general.

In 1897 *Kimpton's Guide* described the post office in glowing terms, noting that 'One cannot fail to admire the imposing building which has been erected at its [the town's] entrance . . . The exterior of the structure – in the semi-Tudor style of architecture – gives, however, but little idea of the spaciousness within, where everything has been done for the health and comfort of the staff, and for a proper discharge of public business.'

The post office today takes up only part of the grand building it occupied formerly. Salter's the newsagents is seen opposite, a striped awning pulled over the window.

High Street

Seemingly unchanging, the High Street
has witnessed many businesses
come and go over the years

Kimpton's was a general store and 'fancy repository'. According to its guide to Arundel from about 1900, items on sale included 'Basket & Wicker Work, Chairs, Tables, Sofas, Flower Stands, Travelling Hampers, and every kind of Artistic and useful Basket Work in stock or made to order. Photos of Arundel. View Books & Guides. Churns of every description of Dairy and Wood Ware.

Kimpton's shop is shown on the far right of the picture. The pump in the middle of the town square was replaced in 1921 by the war memorial, paid for by public subscription.

HIGH STREET, ARUNDEL.   Valentines Series

A winter scene from 1908.

Cane Window Blinds of the best quality at greatly reduced prices. Brooms, Brushes, Mats etc. Cricket Bats, Balls, etc. High-class tobaccos and cigars, walking sticks, purses, toys, dolls and other fancy goods.'

Kimpton's was demolished at the beginning of the 20th century and replaced by the Capital and Counties Bank (now Lloyds Bank). In 1901, the bank manager was Edward Weale. Further up the High Street, on the opposite side, was the London, County and Westminster Bank, which in 1901 was managed by Mr J. Durstan.

Along the road from Kimpton's was Alfred Pain's shop, which was built in the early 1890s. By 1900 he was advertising himself as an 'ironmonger, plumber, gas-fitter, bell-hanger, oil, colour and bar iron merchant'. One of the longest running businesses in town, the shop closed in the late 1990s.

We went to Arundel yesterday.

It is a quaint old town. The road shown in the picture is very steep. We went over part of the Castle.

Yours JPD

3 August 1919
24 Norfolk Road
Littlehampton

Next to the mock Tudor Capital and Counties Bank in the foreground. is Cove's the sweet shop, featuring Rowntree's chocolate in its window. Further up, a rooftop anvil advertises Pain's the ironmongers.

High Street

Built by the Duke, and named after him,
the Norfolk Arms quickly became
Arundel's premier hotel

Before the town hall was built, the Norfolk Arms Hotel was used for town meetings and, on at least one occasion, for a concert. Reputedly haunted, it has long been popular with visitors.

High Street   Arundel

The Norfolk Arms Hotel was built by Charles, the 10th Duke in the early 1780s at a cost of over £7,000. For the first part of its life, the majority of its visitors were troops en route to Portsmouth to take part in the Napoleonic War.

During the early 19th century the Norfolk Arms was the most important hotel in town, catering for families and tourists as well as for commercial travellers. By 1900, John Hare, the proprietor, was providing an omnibus to meet each train and bring guests to the hotel. Visitors could also obtain tickets for the duke's dairy and the castle keep from the hotel, and could hire horses and carriages 'of every description'.

Opposite the Norfolk Arms was the Red Lion commercial inn. In 1900 the proprietor, John E. Ellwood, sold 'Constables' Arundel ales & stouts & wines & spirits of the finest order'. He also offered 'Luncheons, dinners, teas' and 'every accommodation for cyclists'.

On the corner of the High Street and Tarrant Street was the large glass fronted shop of Watts and Nephew. In 1900 they advertised themselves as 'silk mercers, general drapers, milliners, costume & mantle makers, outfitters, hosiers, boat & shoe warehousemen. Undertakers & funeral furnishers'.

The three chaps in boaters outside the Red Lion, on the left, seem posed for the camera. Watts and Nephew were 'High Class Milliners and Costumiers. Ladies' and Gentlemen's Tailors'.

I am just off to Sheffield for a few days. It will be a nice change. I won't be able to write this week as we are having a large party there for the week.

Hope to hear from you soon.

Love from Bella
1 October 1905

Watts and Nephew is in the foreground. Denton's (far left) was the Arundel Tea Exchange and Provision Warehouse in 1900. J.G. Denton also had a shop in South Street, Worthing.

19

High Street

The West Sussex Gazette started life
in Arundel, providing both news and
employment for the town

In 1853, T.H. Woods, a local printer, and his son William Woods
Mitchell founded *Mitchell's Monthly Advertiser and West Sussex
Market and Railway Intelligencer*. The son became the editor and
the paper was printed in Arundel. After progressing through a
number of different titles and formats, the newspaper evolved into
The West Sussex Gazette.

Following a fire in 1899 that destroyed the workshops and
machines, the premises were rebuilt in an elaborate mock Tudor
style and new machinery was installed. The paper is still printed on
a weekly basis, although the office moved to Chichester during the
late 1990s.

In the
foreground is
the mock
Tudor frontage
of the *West
Sussex
Gazette*
offices. Note
how the two
vehicles
further up the
road are
parked
sideways
because of
the gradient.

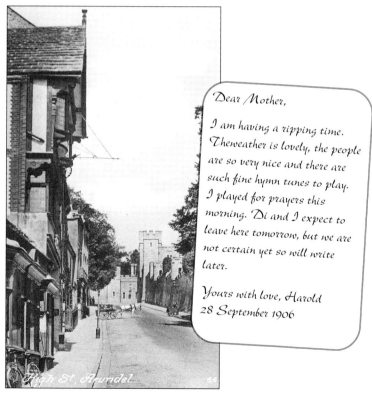

Dear Mother,

*I am having a ripping time.
The weather is lovely, the people
are so very nice and there are
such fine hymn tunes to play.
I played for prayers this
morning. Di and I expect to
leave here tomorrow, but we are
not certain yet so will write
later.*

Yours with love, Harold
28 September 1906

HIGH STREET, ARUNDEL, OPPOSITE POST OFFICE.

John Salter's shop was a 'fancy repository' as well as a newsagents.

Lapworth's shop, known locally as 'Lappie's' was a newsagents, stationers, printers and 'fancy goods store'. For some youngsters, like F.W.G. Clifton, it was their idea of heaven, as the shop sold a number of different comics including the *Marvel*, the *Magnet* and *Comic Cuts* as well as toys and children's books.

A.W. Lapworth and his son Percy also sold tourist and souvenir goods including picture postcards, and they ran a profitable printing business on the premises. They used a gas engine to power the printer as the majority of the town wasn't supplied with electricity until the 1930s.

HIGH ST., ARUNDEL.

Lapworth. The Arundel Stationery and Fancy Goods Store.

Lapworth's Arundel Stationery and Fancy Goods Store. Mr Lapworth is standing in the doorway. The building carries a sign for Lipton's teas.

Maltravers Street

One of the grandest streets in town,
it housed both rich and poor and provided
places of entertainment and detention

Maltravers Street has formed one of the principal roads in Arundel since an early date. In the beginning of the 15th century, it was known as Old Chipping (or Chepynge) Street, so called because of the markets held there. A century later, it had changed to Old Market Street and by the early 19th century, it had gained its current name. By the middle of the 18th century, the street had become one of the most select residential parts of town and was

These two views (one from the early 20th century, the other from the early 21st century), show how little has changed – apart from the traffic.

Arundel.　　　　　*Maltraver's Street.*

The Wrench Series, No. 20307

known locally as White Waistcoat Street, in recognition of the number of professional people who lived there.

At the beginning of the 19th century, Henry Thornton established a theatre in Maltravers Street. Although it attracted local people such as the Duke of Norfolk, as well as some from further afield, plays did not take place on a regular basis, and by 1840 the theatre had closed down. In 1911 *Pike's Local Directory* stated that there was a free library in Maltravers Street. It had opened in 1906. The site was given by the duke, and the building was paid for by Andrew Carnegie. The library had some 4,000 books. The reading room was open daily between 9.30am and 9pm, while the lending library opened between 10am and 1pm and then again between 6pm and 9pm.

In the mid 19th century, improvements to the road took place to reduce its gradient and widen the street. The parade to the north was also built about this time. Despite these changes, the steepness of the road still posed a challenge to vehicles. One woman remembered that during the 1930s 'lorries changed gear three times outside on the gradient up to the main part of Maltravers Street'.

On the right, flying a flag, is the town hall. Nearer the camera on the right is the old police station, established in the 1890s. In the 1970s it moved to its present position in the Causeway.

Maltravers Street

Built in the 1830s, the sombre town hall
provided gaiety and amusement as well as
a home for the fire brigade

Duke Henry built these almshouses in the early 1880s. Further along the road the start of the north parade can be seen.

Among the grand houses and places of entertainment, the street also provided housing for some of the poor of the town. In the early 1880s, almshouses designed by J.A. Hansom and paid for by Henry, the 15th duke, were built at Nos. 40 to 44. On the corner of the building a statue of Emperor Henry II, Duke Henry's patron saint, was erected.

The almshouses at the junction of Maltravers Street and School Lane.

In 1887, in celebration of Queen Victoria's golden jubilee, two other almshouses were built in Maltravers Street, on the junction with School Lane. The Duke of Norfolk and local people contributed the funds to build the cottages.

The rather grim looking town hall in Maltravers

Street was designed by Robert Abraham and built in the early 1830s. It replaced the old town hall which had stood in the High Street, opposite the Norfolk Hotel. *Kimpton's Guide to Arundel* described the new town hall as 'built in the Norman style, bearing the badges of the Howard Lion, the Fitzalan Horse and the Borough Arms – a swallow volant'.

As well as its official use as a court and a place of detention, public events such as concerts and balls were held at the town hall. The town fire brigade with its hand operated fire engine was also based there. In 1911 *Pike's Local Directory* noted that the brigade consisted of 16 firemen under Captain O. Evershed and Lieutenant E.F. Farrington.

J.A. Hansom of Hansom cab fame designed these mock-Tudor buildings in the 1880s. They replaced a much earlier butcher's shop.

. Town Hall

In addition to its three basement cells and courtroom, the town hall had a large upstairs room that was used for civic functions as well as plays and concerts.

The College

The 14th century college today survives
in many forms, both religious and secular

St Nicholas church was originally part of the college that housed a
group of secular clergy known as canons. Built around an open
courtyard, the college buildings included a kitchen and refectory on
the east, cloisters on the west, a master's house, chapel and living
quarters for the canons.

During the 16th century some of the buildings were destroyed,
although the chapel, master's house, kitchen wing and part of the
cloisters survived. From the mid-18th century onwards repairs and
alterations were made to the buildings, resulting in a variety of new
uses over the years, including a convent, school and theatre.

In the early 19th century, the 14th Duke of Norfolk repaired
some of college buildings and turned part of them into a convent
for Carmelite nuns. In 1861, the Sisters of the Servite Order
succeeded the Carmelites. As well as their convent, which was

Aerial view
showing the
remains of
the college
buildings and
St Nicholas
church.

Miss K Graham

*I hope that you are feeling all the better for your
holiday. I hope the weather is nice. It is lovely here.*

*Love from Nina
25 September 1913*

called St Winifred's, the nuns ran a school in the college, which was known as the Priory.

By 1960, the convent and school had closed and the Priory was used as a children's home. This in turn was converted into sheltered housing for the elderly, and the Priory Playhouse was built at the end of the building where once there had been a chapel.

Entrance to the sheltered housing, formerly part of the convent.

Arundel.

The Convent.

A view of the convent school from the early 20th century. The building in the foreground is now the Priory Playhouse.

St Nicholas Church

Dating from the 14th century, this building
contains two churches of different religions

There has been a church on the site of St Nicholas since Saxon
times. During the 14th century the church was neglected and fell
into ruins. Nothing is left of this older church as its stones were
used in the building of the new church in 1380. One of the original
stones, engraved with four crosses, can be seen in the porch.

At the same time that the church was built the religious college
of the Holy Trinity, Our Lady and All Saints was established next
to it. Although they were part of the same building, an iron grille
divided the parish church from the college chapel (which is now
known as the Fitzalan Chapel). Conditions inside the church were
basic, with a mud floor covered in rushes or straw. There was no
seating in the main body of the church, only a stone seat running
along the walls. The walls were painted: when whitewash was
removed in the 19th century several medieval paintings were
discovered. The townspeople were expected to go to church
regularly, although few of them could understand the services as
they were held in Latin.

During the dissolution of the monasteries in the 16th century,
the college was sold to Henry Fitzalan, Earl of Arundel. While the

A view of the church dating from the early 20th century. The part of it to the right of the tower is the Fitzalan Chapel.

St. Nicholas Church, Arundel

parish church continued to hold services, the college chapel fell into disrepair and some of the college buildings were destroyed.

During the Civil War, parliamentary soldiers used the church as a barracks and the Fitzalan Chapel for stabling their horses, causing a great deal of damage to both. Cannons were taken to the top of the church tower to fire on the castle. The barbican tower of the castle still bears the marks of the cannon balls.

The interior of the church looking towards the altar and, beyond that, the Fitzalan Chapel.

Dear E

We are having a nice times. It's very pretty here. I hope to write to you when I get home. Laura is waiting to be off so can't write any more.

With love Agg

The entrance to the church. The postcard, which is dated 31 January 1913 on the back, was published by W.A. Lapworth, who had a shop in the High Street.

The Fitzalan Chapel

Founded in 1380, the chapel is still used
by the Norfolk family as a place of prayer
and burial

View of the
Fitzalan
Chapel
looking
towards the
impressive
stained glass
window.

Richard, 4th Earl of Arundel, established the Fitzalan Chapel in
1380. It was originally the chancel of the medieval church and the
college chapel. As part of their daily duties the secular canons of
the college said prayers in the chapel for the souls of the dead earls
and their families.

Already in a state of disrepair after the dissolution of the
monasteries, the chapel was further damaged during the Civil War.
It was badly neglected in the following 150 years and suffered
more damage, including the destruction of the original timber roof.

Work to restore the chapel started in the 19th century. In the late
19th century a court ruled that the Fitzalan Chapel was a separate
religious entity and did not form part of the parish church. This
decision resulted in an extremely rare situation – that of a Roman
Catholic chapel and an Anglican parish church sharing the same
building.

For centuries the chapel has housed the tombs of numerous
earls of Arundel and dukes of Norfolk. It is still used as a burial
place, and several times a year masses are said for the souls of
the dead, thus continuing the tradition that was started by the
chapel's founder.

Convent of the Poor Clares

Often overlooked, the convent has existed for more than
a century and is part of Arundel's religious life

In 1882 Flora, the Duchess of Norfolk, contacted the poor Clares
in Notting Hill, London, to ask if a convent could be established at
Arundel. This was agreed,and four years later a group of 10 nuns
arrived at Arundel station. They were met by the Duke and Duchess
and made either way up the hill to their new home at Crossbush.
The convent was built on land donated by Henry, the 15th duke,
and Flora contributed to the cost of the building.

The order of St Clare was founded in the early 13th century and
was based on the life and teachings of St Francis of Assisi. St Clare
called her order 'poor' in recognition of their vow of poverty.

CONVENT OF POOR CLARES, ARU

*I asked if I might send you this photograph (which will suffice
until you see for yourself how much nicer it is) of "home". Your
postcard arrived on the 17th, the very day on which I was given the
blessed cord of St Francis, making me a Franciscan, to wear whilst
still a postulant! Mine is only until I become a Poor Clare. Very
much love to you all. You are allowed to come! Love A.*

The Cathedral

Dominating the town's skyline,
the cathedral started life as a parish church

The imposing Roman Catholic church on London Road, was the idea of Henry, the 15th Duke of Norfolk. Work started in 1869 and the building was opened on 1 July 1873. The designer, J.A. Hansom, who built the church in the French Gothic style, was also responsible for a number of other buildings in Arundel and for inventing the Hansom cab. As Henry had attended the Oratory School in Birmingham, he named his church after St Philip Neri, the Italian priest who had founded the Oratorians in the 16th century.

In the 1930s, St Philip's was described as 'our very beautiful and well-loved parish church'. In 1965, the church became the cathedral for the Arundel and Brighton diocese and was renamed the cathedral of Our Lady and St Philip.

A vew of the cathedral looking along the London Road from the town.

Arundel Cathedral.

In 1971, following the canonization of St Philip Howard, his remains were moved from the Fitzalan Chapel to the cathedral, where a shrine to him was built. Queen Elizabeth I imprisoned St Philip, the 13th Earl of Arundel, in the Tower of London because of his faith.

After eleven years in the Tower, St Philip died there in 1595, aged 38. The cathedral was rededicated to him in 1973, and became the cathedral of Our Lady and St Philip Howard.

Dear F

Arrived 11-15, safely with pictures.
Am going to develop the plates.
Will let you know how they come out.

As always, Percy
20 June 1904

Arundel, St. Phillip's Church.

Although the cathedral took only three years to complete, the planned 280ft spire was not built because of problems with the foundations.

16   ARUNDEL. - Church of St. Philip Neri, Interior. — LL.

A view towards the altar, showing the cathedral's wonderful architecture.

33

The Cathedral

Introduced in 1877, the Corpus Christi
celebrations have become a highlight
of the town's year

A colourful event in the cathedral's
calendar is the carpet of flowers which is
part of the Corpus Christi celebrations.
Henry, the 15th Duke, introduced these
celebrations in 1877 after having seen
them in Italy. They mark the Feast of the
Blessed Sacrament.

The cathedral is decorated with a carpet
of flowers along the length of the aisle, and
on Corpus Christi a procession makes its
way from the cathedral to the castle, where
an open-air benediction is held.

Apart from a break during the First
World War, the celebrations have been
held every year since 1877, and they
continue to be a popular event with both
locals and tourists.

The design of the carpet of flowers
changes every year and is kept a closely
guarded secret by those working on it.

The cathedral
decorated
with the
carpet of
flowers for
Corpus
Christi.

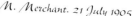

Dearest C

Arrived home safely – aftr a most enjoyable week. Love to dear self.

M. Merchant. 21 July 1905

Two views from 1905 showing the procession coming down London Road from the cathedral to the castle.

Dear H,

Have sent logs. Hoping you are all well. Marked boys [on the postcard above]. G is first [the third boy on the postcard]. J is behind.

With love to all, A & GSM
24 July 1905

Duke and Earls

The Dukes of Norfok and Earls of Arundel
are as much a part of the town as their
impressive castle

Arundel Castle, with a portrait of Henry, the 15th Duke of Norfolk. As well as being responsible for extensive works to the castle, the duke also paid for a number of buildings in the town.

ARUNDEL CASTLE, SUSSEX. Copyright. THE DUKE OF NORFOLK.

In 1067, Roger de Montgomery, a kinsman of William the Conqueror who had guarded Normandy while William was fighting in England, was made the first Earl of Arundel. A stone in the town square, quoting an anonymous and undated rhyme, notes that 'Since William rose and Harold fell, there have been Earls at Arundel'.

In the late 1550s Mary, the daughter of Henry, the 12th earl, married Thomas Howard, the 4th Duke of Norfolk. When the duke was later beheaded for plotting against Queen Elizabeth, his titles and lands reverted to the Crown. In 1660, Charles II reinstated Thomas, the 16th Earl of Arundel, as the 5th Duke of Norfolk.

The relationship between the castle and the town depended largely on the personalities of the dukes and earls and whether they chose to make Arundel their home. From the 19th century onwards, the link seems to have been particularly strong. Henry, the 15th duke, was involved in the life of the town, paying for a number of buildings, including the almshouses in Maltravers Street and the Church of England school in Surrey Street. The castle also provided water for the town, and the duke was the postmaster general of the newly built post office.

Special occasions also provided a chance for the town and castle to celebrate together. From the late Victorian period until the Second World War, local children were invited to the castle for a Christmas party. After tea in the servants' hall, they were entertained in the Barons' Hall. Each received a present from the tree, an orange, an apple and a bag of sweets.

In 1929, to mark the 21st birthday of Duke Bernard, a children's party was held at the castle and every child was given a souvenir mug. This relationship continues today, with the town and castle recently joining forces to celebrate the millennium and the Queen's golden jubilee.

Bernard Mamaduke, the Earl of Arundel, with his sisters Lady Rachel and Lady Katherine. He succeeded to the dukedom in 1917, when he was still a child.

~ LADY KATHERINE ~   EARL OF ARUNDEL   LADY RACHEL ~

In 1904 the duke and his new bride, Gwendolen, were welcomed home with a triumphal arch erected at the entrance to the bridge.

The Castle

Designed as a Norman fortification,
the castle started life as a wooden
building on top of a mound of earth

A castle
has been a
dominant
feature of the
Arundel
skyline since
1067. The
first one
would have
been in the
motte and
bailey form
used for
defensive
building at
the time.

In 1067, a year after the Battle of Hastings, William the Conqueror rewarded Roger de Montgomery with land in Sussex, Shropshire and Wales. Like other men granted land by William, Roger had to provide defensive buildings to help the new king maintain his power and to ward off possible attacks.

Roger's fortification was built on high ground overlooking the river Arun, with good views towards the south coast and the Channel. The wooden castle was built on top of a 100ft-high bank of earth. Further earthworks were built to provide protection around the castle, particularly on the western, landward side.

Over the next century the castle was extended and the older, wooden parts were gradually replaced with stone. From about 1070 onwards the gatehouse was built, using stone from Pulborough which was brought to Arundel by river. In about 1140 Caen stone from Normandy was used to replace Roger's wooden keep.

In the late 12th century the castle reverted to the Crown for a while. During this time Henry II paid for work to various parts of the castle, including the chapel and the herb garden. Despite later developments and restorations, some of the king's work still survives today.

In the late 13th century Edward I granted Richard, the first Fitzalan Earl of Arundel, the right to hold two fairs a year. Richard was allowed to levy a tax on goods sold at the fairs, and he used this new income to refurbish and improve the castle. The well tower and the new barbican in front of the Norman gateway date from this period.

Richard, the 3rd Earl of Arundel, continued the building work started by his grandfather. Richard was a wealthy man and he used the keep as his treasury. As the castle was his principal home, he expanded the buildings to meet his needs and to provide lodgings and workspaces for his growing retinue of servants. He also obtained permission to establish a college of secular priests at Arundel, although it was his son who carried out this project, along with further works to the castle.

Changes continued to be made during the 14th, 15th and 16th centuries, although signs of decay were beginning to appear. By the 1630s some parts of the castle, including the keep and hall, were described as being in a poor state and in need of repair.

ARUNDEL CASTLE, FROM THE NORTH WEST.

The 100ft-high motte can be seen in the left foreground, with the stone keep on top. The Norman gatehouse and 13th century barbican are in the centre of the picture.

39

The Castle

Besieged during the Civil War, the castle was in a poor state when Charles began his restoration works

The castle keep before restoration work which started at the beginning of the 20th century.

In 1643, during the Civil War, the castle was besieged first by Royalist troops loyal to the king and then by Roundhead troops under the command of General Waller. The castle was damaged during the fighting, and when the Roundhead troops withdrew they blew up parts of the fortifications.

In the years after the Civil War parts of the castle deteriorated through lack of attention. As successive dukes of Norfolk chose to stay away from the castle it became a place of romantic ruins and for storing furniture rather than a family home. At one stage the keep, which had once been a treasury, was used to house a number of owls.

Charles, the 11th Duke, began major restoration works from 1787 onwards, with the aim of recreating the medieval castle. As Francis Hiorne, the proposed architect, died before the work had begun, Charles drew up the plans himself. His work was widely criticised, and much of it was later destroyed. Today only a few parts of his buildings, including the library, survive.

The next large building phase occurred from the 1870s onwards, when Henry, the 15th Duke, incorporated new designs by Charles Buckler. The project continued until the beginning of the 20th century,and most of what can be seen today is Henry's work.

40

We're having a splendid time down here.
I wish you were with me.

Much love, Dorothy

7 September 1908

The Courtyard, Arundel Castle

Parts of the quadrangle date from the 12th century, although most of the buildings were rebuilt or restored during the 18th and 19th centuries.

Arundel Castle; Courtyard.

The courtyard and keep. When Queen Victoria and Prince Albert stayed here in 1846 a large sign reading 'Welcome Victoria and Albert' was illuminated by gas as their carriage entered the quadrangle.

Inside the castle

From wooden fort to royal guest house,
the castle gradually evolved into a place
equipped with all the latest mod cons

The grand staircase was rebuilt in the Victorian period. It contains both religious and secular imagery, including the Nativity and heraldic beasts from the Norfolk coat of arms.

Grand Staircase, Arundel Castle.

Although built as a means of defence, Arundel castle was also home to generations of earls and dukes. Over the years, the interior was improved to provide comfortable living quarters for the family and work areas for the household servants. Gradually it was filled with furniture, paintings and other decorative features.

By the end of the 16th century the furnishings included tapestries and other hangings, Turkish carpets, gold and silver embroidered coats of arms, velvet cushions, oak cupboards and a range of other household goods including bed linen and chamber pots.

Important guests also provided an opportunity for adding to the comfort of the castle. In December 1846, Queen Victoria and Prince Albert stayed at the castle for three days. In preparation for their visit, the 13th duke, who had been told of their visit well in advance, set to work upgrading the interior. According to the *Illustrated London News*, this work was in 'a style of gorgeous magnificence'. In particular, the duke provided a suite of rooms for his royal guests that had 'regal splendour' and were decorated in a rich but tasteful style. The overall impression was a 'remarkably pleasing and elegant effect'.

One of the many corridors of Arundel Castle.

In the 1880s the castle, which had sometimes proved difficult to warm, was installed with central heating. At the end of the 19th century a guide to Arundel noted that 'the electric lighting of the whole of the interior has been successfully accomplished'. The generating station was installed in a mock Tudor building on the London Road. Other innovations included service lifts, a ventilator for the kitchen, fire-fighting equipment and extensive drainage and plumbing throughout the castle. By the start of the 20th century, Arundel could proudly boast that its castle was one of the few in the country that was fitted with every 'modern' convenience.

The Great or Barons' Hall was rebuilt in the late Victorian period on the site of the medieval hall. During this work central heating was installed under the floor.

Inside the castle

Widely rebuilt in the late Victorian period,
the castle still retains older styles
and glimpses of earlier tastes

The library, in
the Gothic
styles, is one
of the few
remaining
pieces of
work by
Charles, the
11th duke.
It houses
some 10,000
books, many
of which he
collected.

The Library, Arundel Castle.

Originally
used as a
private
chapel, the
room was
converted
into a dining
room in the
late 18th
century.

The Dining Hall, Arundel Castle.

The drawing room is dominated by a magnificent fireplace, displaying numerous heraldic devices.

In the late 1870s the 15th duke rebuilt the drawing room on the site of the medieval great hall.

45

The Castle Lodges

Built as entrances rather than for defence,
the lodges and gateways help to define
the castle's grounds

Two views of
the South or
Lower
Lodge.
It was
designed by
Charles
Buckler and
was built in
the late 19th
century.

New Entrance Lodge, Arundel Castle

Dear Win

*At the park enjoying ourselves. It
is a splendid place. Arrived to the
minute 12.20.*

Love Sid, 6 August 1905

South Entrance, Arundel Castle

Swanbourne Lodge, overlooking the lake, was designed by William Burn and built in the 19th century.

Whiteways Lodge, at the northern end of the park, was built at the end of the 18th century as part of Charles's work to extend and enclose the park.

William Burn designed this entrance lodge, completed in the middle of the 19th century, at the top of the High Street. The gateway carries heraldic devices.

The Park

Created from downland and a rabbit warren,
the park has witnessed celebrations, battles
and the burial of a giant

Charles, the 11th Duke, created the new park in the late 18th
century as part of his plans to restore the castle and its grounds. He
bought over 1,100 acres of land to the north of the castle to form
the park. Part of this land was covered by an extensive rabbit
warren, known as Pugh Dean, reputedly the burial place of Bevis,

During the
First World
War the
Canadian
troops who
were based
in the park
were allowed
to shoot the
deer.

In 1900 it
was noted
that there
were several
pea-fowl in
the park by
Swanbourne
Lodge, 'some
of which are
albinos, very
curious to
behold'.

PEACOCKS IN ARUNDEL PARK.

the legendary giant associated with the castle. The warren was destroyed and the park was planted with beech and other trees.

A flint and brick wall stretching over several miles marked some of the park boundaries and lodges, such as Whiteways Lodge, were built around the perimeter. Swanbourne Lake was enlarged and deer were introduced. By 1900, there were about 1,000 fallow deer, a herd of red deer and, by Hiorne's Tower, there was a small herd of Brahmin cattle. In nearby paddocks there were llamas, rheas and ostriches.

Apart from a short period under the 13th duke, the park has been open to the public since its creation. It has also been used to hold a number of special events over the years. In 1897, as part of Queen Victoria's diamond jubilee celebrations, more than 3,500 school children attended a fete in the park. Each child received tea as well as a medal and a souvenir mug.

Hiorne's Tower was built in 1790 by Francis Hiorne for the 11th Duke. Designed in a Gothic revival style, the triangular building was intended as a model for the restoration of the castle. As Hiorne died two years later, the duke carried out the work to the castle according to his own design.

Easter Sunday, 1920

I'm here again! No, this is not a Sunday ramble but a weekend. Why don't you come down too?

Kind regards, E Mayo

Hiorne Tower, Arundel Park.

Although Francis Hiorne died two years after building his tower, his name lives on in the park.

The Park

A scene of pageants and festivals, the park
also offered walking and alfresco dining

In 1923
a large
historical
pageant was
held to raise
money for
the local
hospitals.

Pughdean Hill. Arundel Park.

PUGHDEAN HILL, ARUNDEL PARK.

Where Lilian, Stephen and I spent a lovely spring afternoon, after a picnic by Swanbourne Lake, having walked from Littlehampton.

24 April 1913

The Park

In peacetime and in war the park was home
to thousands of troops over the years

A regular feature of park life were the military camps held there.
The soldiers came from the regular army as well as volunteer and
territorial units. In 1860 more than 3,000 spectators turned out to
watch a mock battle in the park, and during the Second World War
troops and tanks were based there.

The soldiers
taking part in
the camps
included
many from
Sussex,
Surrey and
Kent.

On the back of this postcard, sent in August 1905, Frank points out that it shows the officers of his regiment. In the middle, with the beard, is the Duke of Norfolk.

Arundel Park, Monday night

Could not get to Post Office today but will tomorrow. I went to the Black Rabbit tonight by boat, 1¼ hrs of boat for 6d so was very nice.

It has been very nice here today, sunshine this afternoon. Am having an easy time of it. Have done practically nothing all day bar examine a few recruits.

Sid, 13 July 1909

Church parade in the park, 1909.

Swanbourne Lake

Beautiful and useful, the lake provided power,
water and recreation for the town

Swanbourne Lake started life as a millpond that was in existence
by the time of the Domesday survey in the 11th century. In the late
18th century, during work to the park, the pond was enlarged to
form the lake.

For centuries the lake provided water to power the mill and to
supply the castle and town. In 1835 a flint and brick pump house,
designed by Robert Abraham, was built near the lake. At first the
pumping engine was driven by water from the lake before switching
to gas and then diesel.

The lake is fed by 'Blue Springs', which get their name from
the colour of the water as it comes out of the ground. Most of the
water comes from rain falling on the South Downs. Some of it is
intercepted before it reaches the lake and is used to supply a
number of other towns, including Littlehampton and Worthing.

A place of great beauty, the lake has long been a favourite resort
for walks, boating, picnics and feeding the ducks. Nowadays over
100,000 people are drawn to this picturesque spot every year. A
large variety of animals and plants are to be found around the lake,
including a number of rare and endangered species.

View of the
lake looking
towards Mill
Road.

Swanbourne Lake, Arundel Park.

One Arundel woman recalled that some of the celebrations for the wedding of the duke and duchess in 1904 were held at the lake: 'We had fireworks at Swanbourne Lake . . . We wore evening dress – or rather the grown-ups did – and went out by a boat to a little island in the centre of Swanbourne after dark.'

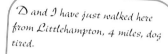

D and I have just walked here from Littlehampton, 4 miles, dog tired.

Love Daisy

5 August 1911

During the First World War a German aircraft crashed into the lake. One of its defused bombs is on display in the castle.

View across the lake towards Swanbourne Lodge, which was built in the middle of the 19th century. Gertie's card, sent in 1904, says it all.

Swanbourne Lake

A long-established environment for wildlife, the lake provides a safe haven for many endangered species

Tranquil scenes from the early 1910s.

SWANBOURNE LAKE, ARUNDEL.

This is a pretty little spot. Had tea by this lake the other afternoon. We have had such a delightful holiday I feel quite sorry to leave it all.

J E H, 10 August 1905

Swanbourne Lake & Arundel Castle.

In 1947 Francis D. Allison described the millstream as being 'once almost as famous for trout as the Arun was for mullet. The walks along its banks on either side through green woods that lead to the Arun are a dream of loveliness.'

Today visitors can feed the trout in the circular millpond that was converted to a trout farm in 1987.

Ye Olde Water Mill, Swanbourne Lake, Arundel

An artist's impression of the water mill as it might have been when John Constable painted it and the castle.

I thought you would like a bit of Arundel for your collection. It is really beautiful here, so many nice walks one could stay a long time. Hoping you are keeping well. With love from S.

5 August 1908

The Mill Stream, Arundel.

The mill stream leading down to the river Arun.

The Dairy

Admired by Queen Victoria, the dairy provided
milk for the castle and the town
and was popular with tourists

Built in 1845, the dairy was designed by Robert Abraham for the 13th duke. It was erected on the site of the water mill that had been demolished a few years earlier. The dairy formed part of a group of buildings that included a cowshed, pumphouse and a farmhouse for the dairyman.

According to *Kimpton's Guide to Arundel* the butter in the dairy was churned by water power. A hand churn can be seen through the archway to the left of the dairy.

The buidings from left to right are the dairy, the barn and cowshed and the pumphouse. Out of the picture to the left is the farmhouse.

At Duke's Dairy, Arundel

From the early 1890s the dairy produced milk, butter and cream for the castle. Any surplus was given to the poor of the town.

The dairy was designed as an octagonal building with a lantern roof. Inside, blue and white tiles and a fountain kept it cool. Queen Victoria praised the newly opened dairy during her visit to the town in 1846. Three years after her visit it was opened to the public.

A tourist guide from 1900 noted that the dairy 'may be freely viewed, on Mondays and Fridays, from Twelve to Four. Tickets obtainable at the Norfolk Arms Hotel'. The guide described the dairy as having 'seven windows through which the light shows to advantage its unrivalled cleanliness and tasteful arrangements with marble troughs, sparkling fountain and exquisitely-carved tables of marble after the model of the Queen's Dairy, Windsor'. It closed to the public in the early 1930s.

A view of the farmhouse with its rather grand garden and fountain.

The Black Rabbit

Set on the banks of the river Arun among
beautiful scenery, the inn has been
a popular spot for a hundred years

The Black Rabbit started life as a row of workmen's cottages. During the middle of the 19th century the inn was widely used by navvies working on the railway and the waterways and became notorious as a place for drunkenness and brawling.

By the beginning of the 20th century the inn's reputation had improved and it had become a popular riverside spot with both townspeople and visitors. In an advert in *Kimpton's Popular Guide to Arundel* from about 1900, the inn was described as 'commanding a beautiful view of the Castle and River'.

In 1900 the proprietor, Daniel Lee, was able to offer a 'Dancing saloon, croquet grounds, swings . . . luncheons, dinners, teas'. Other amusements included archery, bowls and boat trips. Despite the strength of the river currents, Mr Lee hired out small rowing boats, a practice that was continued by Sam Knight, his successor.

The Black Rabbit is apparently the only pub of this name in the country. The origin of the name is uncertain. It has been suggested that a black rabbit was a good sign: it showed gamekeepers that poachers were not around, as a black rabbit would have been an obvious, and therefore easy, target.

Early 20th century view from above the Black Rabbit.

Dear Mrs Tucknott

Arrived safely. It is pouring with rain while writing this card so you can guess what we feel like.

Love from Daisy
August 1923

Views of the inn, with boats for hire.

BLACK RABBIT, ARUNDEL

Dear Miss B

I hope you get plenty of dancing tonight.

W. A. Arundel 1905

ARUNDEL.   The Black Rabbit.

61

Around Arundel

Most of the places mentioned in the book are within walking distance of the town centre. Arundel is a compact town, and you can see many of the sights by taking a circular tour of the main streets. For those wanting a longer walk, Arundel Park is extensive and contains many beautiful areas. A stroll down Mill Road or along the river Arun leads to the Black Rabbit. In summer, pleasure boats run trips to the pub from the town quay.

A picture of the water woods sent on 26 May 1923 in which Douglas asks his aunt to send his football socks and 'any spirals you can grab'.

London Road looking towards the cathedral. The white building in front is the St Mary's Gate inn, which dates back to the 16th century.

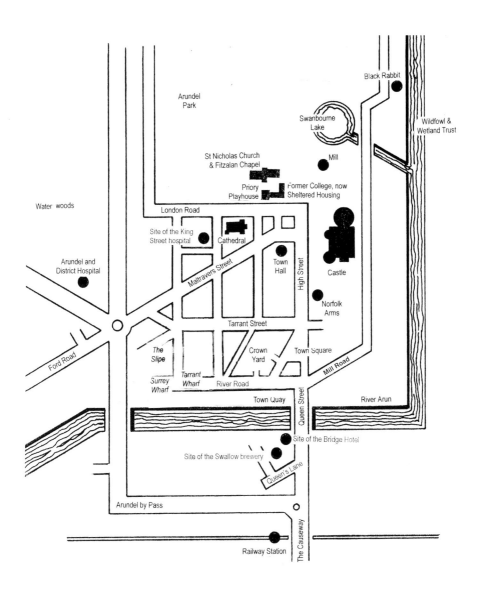

Index